How to Make
Papier Mâché
Sculptures

Sculptures & Creations

Incorporating Household Waste

Rachaël Fillâtre

Published in 2017 by

Createspace Publishing

©Rachael Fillâtre 2017

ISBN-13:
978-1542688444

ISBN-10:
1542688442

Created by Rachaël Fillâtre

TABLE OF CONTENTS

"The purpose of art is washing the dust of daily life off our souls". Pablo Picasso.

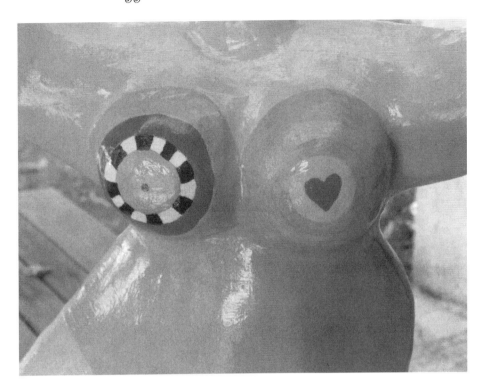

INTRODUCTION

Would you like to help the environment and at the same time create fun art objects for your home? Do you have old, worn out clothes, broken crockery and piles of stuff to recycle? Before you throw anything out consider transforming it and using it to decorate your home.

Each project in this book uses items that we would normally throw away. There are so many different ways to extend the usefulness of paper, plastic, cans, glass, clothing, and other objects destined for the bin.

1

The possibilities for upcycling are endless. Here you will find plenty of ideas and inspiration for giving value to trash.

In an issue of *Entrepreneur*, Jennifer Wang says that "the best way to think of upcycling is that it's like a sexier, even greener version of recycling." And, author and Professor Reiner Pilz coined the term upcycling, saying that "recycling is technically down-cycling. They smash bricks; they smash everything, causing it to decrease in value. What we need is upcycling where old products are given more value not less."

Although I aspire to the likes of Bea Johnson in *Zero Waste Home*, I am not quite there. I still seem to have an awful lot of stuff to get rid of. Therefore, while I am waiting to become zero waste perfect, I tart up my trash! That is, I turn my trash into treasure. Almost everything can be revamped or reinvented.

As I am a paper mache freak ("papier mâché" in proper French terms), I create my objects and sculptures using this fabulous, inexpensive and versatile medium combined with the discarded items themselves.

The projects in this book are mainly aimed at adults and are illustrated with step-by-step instructions and photographs. Listed in advance are the basic materials and equipment you will need.

The beauty of combining art, crafts and upcycling together is the perfect means of creative expression for me and I find the whole process therapeutic and relaxing.

In the words of Friedrich Nietzsche, "Art is the proper task of life."

So let's get on with it!

"Sculpture is the art of the intelligence."

Pablo Picasso

THE PROJECTS

The projects in this book are a guide to what can be done, but the instructions do not need to be followed too strictly, indeed they can be adapted to your own whims.

I hope to get your creative juices flowing by showing you what I did and how I constructed my pieces of work with very little financial outset.

On some objects I have used a combination of paper strips and pulp, but all of these projects can be made by just using the paper strips method, which some people may find easier and less messy.

For each project refer back to both Equipment and Materials and Techniques sections for guidance.

"A guilty conscience needs to confess. A work of art is a confession." Albert Camus.

EQUIPMENT AND MATERIALS

The benefit of using paper mache as a medium is that the materials are inexpensive or virtually free. The basic equipment and materials you will need to undertake these projects are:

Scissors, masking tape, knife, spoon, pencil, paint brushes, sandpaper, rubber gloves, colander, tea-strainer, plastic containers, newspapers, glue, varnish, aluminum foil, paints, glass jars, plaster of Paris, joint powder, a liquidizer (optional), plastic bags, a long stick (bamboo, dowel or branch), and old golf balls, door knobs etc).

In addition to these basic items, I used all sorts of other household waste and junk which will be listed separately for each project.

I recommend using gloves especially as things can get a bit messy and if you choose to use wallpaper paste (as your glue option) it contains chemicals which aren't too kind to the skin. If you do not have a small strainer, any small concave object will do, for example a shallow teacup.

Masking tape can be expensive and I use rather a lot, so I tend to buy in bulk or in DIY centre sales.

A range of paint brushes in different sizes is useful and fine sandpaper works best for these projects, especially when sanding directly onto the paper finish.

The best paints, I find, are acrylic paints and emulsions. Matt emulsion can be used for undercoating and painting larger areas. It is a good way to use up old paints left over from home decorating. However, any type of paint can be used if acrylic or emulsions are not available.

If using water based paints, you may need to adapt your varnish to suit as certain varnishes do not work well with water colours and these types of paints have a tendency to run.

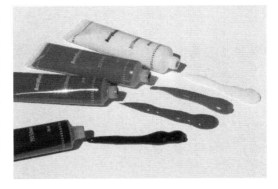

"Art enables us to find ourselves and lose ourselves at the same time." Thomas Merton

BASIC TECHNIQUES

The basic techniques for paper mache are very simple and can be learnt very quickly. There are two main paper mache methods: layering paper strips, and paper pulp.

Glue: there are several glue options:

PVA or white glue: dilute the glue with a little water.

Flour and water: mix together approximately 1 cup of cheap white flour, 1 cup of water and half a teaspoon of salt.

The flour and water paste should have the consistency of single cream. Adjust ingredients accordingly. If you decide to use flour and water, it is a good idea to add a few drops of oil of cloves or oil of wintergreen as this will prevent the object growing mould. Alternatively, a small squirt of household antibacterial cleaner also does the trick.

Wallpaper paste:

If you use wallpaper paste please follow the manufacturer's instructions on the container, however the end product needs to be fairly thin, not too thick.

This type of paste usually contains fungicides so it is handy for avoiding mould, however I would strongly advise using rubber gloves to avoid skin damage. You may be able to purchase a more gentle type of wallpaper paste – they do exist (generally these can be obtained from organic outlets and via the internet).

Paper strips method

Layering strips of paper is the most common method of paper mache. The paper strips are soaked in glue and then added to the object in criss-crossing layers.

For this method you will need to tear up sheets of newspaper (or other lightweight paper) into strips of approximately 10cms x 5cms (roughly 4 x 2 inches).

This is just a rough size guide; you do not have to be strict about it. With practice you will find what works best for you. You will also adapt the size of the strips depending on whether you are working on a large or small area.

The strips should be torn following the direction of the paper grain. Try not to tear against the grain as this makes it difficult to control your tearing and obtain uniform strips.

I recommend not using scissors as torn edges lead to a smoother finish.

Cut edges create lots of ugly lines all over your piece of work.

Using rubber gloves dip the strips into the glue or paste and slide off the excess glue between your fingers.

Each strip will then be applied to the project you are working on.

Continue adding strips. Allow to dry between each layer to avoid having your object buckle and warp as it dries.

I find that about 8 – 10 layers of paper strips are normally enough for the majority of paper mache projects. Layer the paper strips in alternating directions (at a right angle to the previous layer) to make the structure stronger.

Paper pulp method

Paper mache (papier mâché) means "mashed or chewed paper" in French, so the paper pulp method is the truest form of this art in relation to its original and literal meaning.

This differs from the paper strips methods as the paper is actually mashed to make a type of paper clay. It is ideal for covering areas quickly and for sculpting. The downside is that it can take several days to dry. I also add joint powder to my pulp to give extra durability and smoothness.

Here are the instructions for my method:

Add torn pieces of newspaper (approximately 1 sheet of newspaper or 2-3 sheets of A4) to a liquidizer (preferably an old one you don't wish to use for food) and fill with water.

I use very fine newspaper or paper for my projects. For slightly thicker paper, pre-soaking overnight is preferable.

Liquidize the contents for about 10–15 seconds, or until the paper turns to pulp. Pour the contents into an old sieve.

With a spoon squeeze out most of the water, but not all of it.

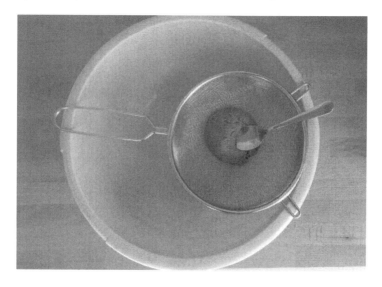

The pulp needs to remain moist enough to mix with the joint powder.

In a plastic container mix the paper pulp with approximately 2 tablespoons of joint powder (the type used for interior wall tiles).

Mix thoroughly.   This is now ready to be applied to your sculpture.

I only make up small batches of this pulp mixture as it tends to dry out quite quickly.

If you do not have a liquidizer (or an electric whisk) to break down the paper it's not a problem, this can be done by hand with a potato masher or similar. Or, alternatively, skip this step and continue with paper strips.

"Every production of an artist should be the expression of an adventure of his soul."
W. Somerset Maugham

Niki Nana

Inspired by Franco-American artist, Niki de St Phalle

NIKI NANA

In addition to the basic materials you will need a stick, plastic tub, a small ball and some plastic bags.

Step 1 – The Base

For the base fill a large plastic yoghurt pot or cream container with plaster of Paris and water (follow manufacturer instructions for amounts) and as the mixture starts to set insert a stick into the middle and push to the bottom. Hold the stick for a few minutes until the plaster starts to harden – it usually sets quite quickly. Make sure the stick remains upright. Here I have chosen an old bamboo cane from the garden. It is approximately 21 inches (53 cms) high.

The plastic carton is approximately 3 inches (7.5 cms) deep. The sculpture will, therefore, be around 18 inches (approx 45.5 cms) high. When the plaster is hard the plastic carton can be cut away with a knife or scissors. The plaster may take a few hours to dry out completely, but you may continue with the project.

Alternatively, you can use an existing object as a base. In the past I have used old lamp bases, wooden mug holders, vases and upright multiple toilet roll holders.

Step 2 - The Armature

Fill five plastic shopping bags with screwed up newspaper.

 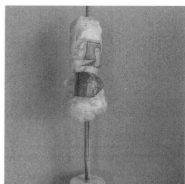

One larger one will be used for the body and four slightly smaller ones for the arms and legs.

If you want the sculpture to be very plump fill the plastic bags quite generously with paper.

Crumple up and tape closed each of the filled bags and attach the largest bag (the body) to the stick with masking tape. Pinch the bag in a little in the middle to form a waist and secure with tape.

Leave a small amount of stick at the top for the head and enough stick at the bottom to form the left leg.

Crumple up each of the other bags into the shapes of arms and legs. To prevent each of them unraveling fix the forms in place with tape. Now attach the limbs to the body and stick.

14

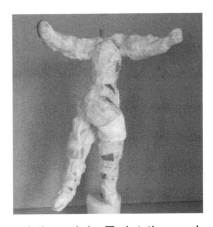

The left leg should be strapped around the stick. Twist the ends of the bags to make hands and feet and secure with tape. To help raise the right leg slightly, insert a small piece of screwed up newspaper as a wedge between the legs. This gives it a bit of lift and prevents the leg wobbling. Tape the wedge in place.

With masking tape attach the golf ball or door knob (or scrunched paper/foil) to the top of the stick to make the head. A small piece of rolled up newspaper or cardboard can be used beforehand to form a neck. Secure with plenty of tape.

Cover the armature as much as possible with masking tape to make it sturdy.

She is now ready for paper machaying!

Step 3 – Adding paper strips

Now for the slightly messy part! Make sure you cover your work surface. Wearing old clothes or an apron is also a good idea.

Cover the whole armature with one layer of paper strips (method shown in Techniques chapter).

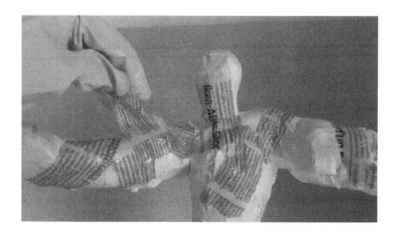

When totally covered leave to dry in an area where there is as much circulating warm air as possible. The drying process can take many hours so ideally leave to dry overnight. You can speed up the process with a hair dryer, but be careful not to get too close to the object.

I usually allow items to dry naturally, in a heated room or outside on a sunny day.

Step 4 – Adding details

You will now need to make breasts and buttocks for your sculpture. To make a mould for each of these, line a tea strainer, a shallow teacup or other similar concave object with a piece of silver foil. Fill this mould with small pieces of screwed up newspaper. When three quarters full, fold over the excess silver foil at the top and seal with masking tape.

You will need to make 4 of these. Depending on the size of your sculpture and your personal taste you can make the buttocks slightly larger if you wish.

Attach these 4 semicircles to the relevant parts of the armature with masking tape.

Make sure the new parts are taped down very securely. Now apply another layer of paper strips over the areas you have just added.

You can also start to cover the base with the strips too. Allow to dry thoroughly.

If you feel that you would like to plump out your chunky lady sculpture even more, for example around the tops of the thighs, the tops of the arms or the waist, fold up dry sheets of newspaper and wrap around the area, securing well with tape.

Cover these areas with more paper strips and glue.

Once this is dry cover the whole sculpture with another 2 layers of paper strips.

Step 5 – Adding paper pulp:

To advance more quickly you can add a layer of paper pulp, but this step is entirely optional (see instructions in Techniques chapter for paper pulp method). You can also achieve a sturdy sculpture just by applying lots of layers of paper strips. As a rough guide a minimum of 8 layers is required.

The paper pulp can be applied with a knife or with your hands. I use a combination of the two. Using gloves is advisable. Spread on to the object to a thickness of about quarter of an inch/half a centimeter.

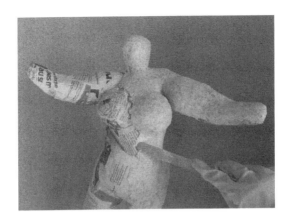

If you still wish to make any areas larger, now is the moment. You can smooth the mixture over certain areas to hide any holes or rough edges. Cover the sculpture completely, including the base, and leave to dry. Once dry, if you find the sculpture is not solid or sturdy enough you may need to add another layer of pulp or more strips.

Step 6 – The finishing touches

Sanding

Once the sculpture is dry, and preferably wearing a protective face mask, sand over any lumps and bumps or creases with a fine sandpaper.

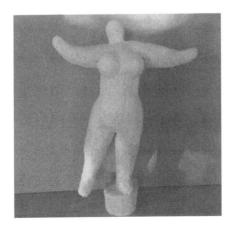

Undercoating

To seal the sculpture, apply two layers of undercoat, using a light coloured emulsion or white acrylic paint.

Painting details

Draw the outline of the swimming costume in pencil, and then paint the background of the costume and the rest of the body in the colours of your choice. You may need two layers of paint for perfect coverage. Once the base coat is dry add any design you wish: spots, stripes, flowers - be as jazzy as you want - anything goes!

Varnishing

When your design is finished, paint on a couple of layers of varnish, allow to dry in between each layer.

"Ah, good taste! What a dreadful thing! Taste is the enemy of creativeness." Pablo Picasso.

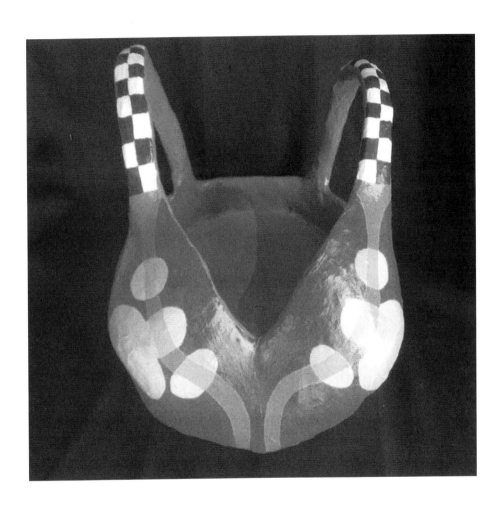

Bra fruit bowl. Inspired by Niki de St Phalle and Pablo Picasso

BRAZIER FRUIT BOWL

This is a fun project and it also makes a great conversation piece.

In addition to the basic equipment and materials you will need an old bra, some medium thickness cardboard and a large plate.

Step 1: The type of bra that works best is one with a slight band under the cups.

Cut a circle out of a piece of cardboard. The circle should be approximately the size of the bottom perimeter of the bra, (i.e. the circumference of your torso).

To make the task easier, I found that a dinner plate was about the same size as the circumference of the bra, I therefore used a plate as a rough template. Depending on your torso, (which you may need to measure), you will need to make the circle larger or smaller than an average size dinner plate.

Step 2: Insert the circle of cardboard into the bottom of the fastened bra, stretching the perimeter of the bra over the sides of the cardboard circle.

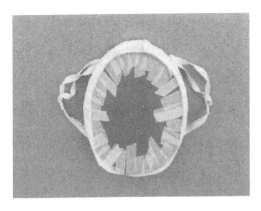

Using tape hold the bra in place on the inside and on the underside of the cardboard.

Step 3: Cover the whole bra (inside and out) with small pieces of masking tape.

It is not necessary to cover the piece of cardboard entirely. The masking tape is to help the paper mache stick to the fabric.

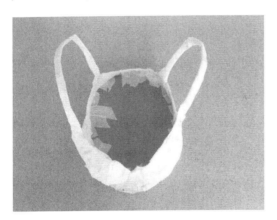

Wrap the masking tape around the bra straps several times. This will stiffen them slightly and make them stand up.

Step 4: Cover the whole bra (inside and out) with three layers of paper mache strips.

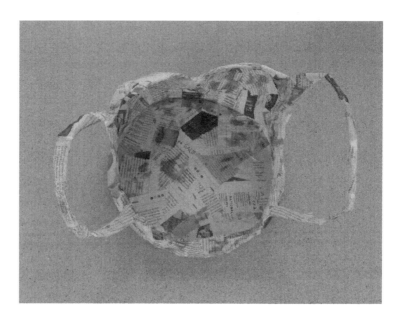

My tip is to not make the paper mache too wet when applying to the bra straps. If the straps are too floppy dry the whole bowl upside down balanced on a large object so that the straps are hanging downwards. Leave the bowl to dry.

Step 5: Cover the underside of the bowl with a layer of paper strips in order to hide the masking tape.

Allow the bowl to dry upside down. I posed this one over a tall paint tin.

Step 6: Next, add a layer of paper pulp to the exterior of the bowl (see pulp recipe and method in Techniques section). Exclude, for now, the bra straps, we will get to them later.

Dry the bowl in a warm room or outside in the sun. The pulp stage is optional, you can, if you wish, continue to add paper strips (approx 8 layers) and leave out the pulp stage completely. I use pulp to advance more quickly, to sculpt and to cover over lumps, bumps and errors.

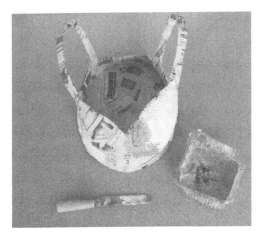

When the exterior of the bowl is dry, add a layer of pulp to the interior of the bra, again leaving the straps until the next stage. There is no particular need to add pulp to the cardboard base of the bowl. This will prevent warping.

Step 7: Place the bowl, once again, over an object and apply the pulp to the inner rim of the straps whilst it is upside down. Make sure pulp is not too watery.

Allow to dry thoroughly as the straps will be fairly fragile.

Step 8: When dry, turn the bowl over and apply a thin layer of pulp to the upper (top) side of the bra strap.

Allow to dry and harden and then add more pulp if necessary.

Step 9: Once the pulp is nice and dry, add one more layer of paper strips.

This layer of paper will give it extra strength and give the bowl a smoother finish.

Step 10: Once dry, lightly sand the surface of the bowl.

Use fine sandpaper so as not to rip the paper. Brush off the dust so that it is clean and smooth for the next stage.

Step 11: Your bowl is now ready for priming and painting. First give it a base coat preferably using a white or light coloured emulsion or acrylic paint to conceal the newsprint.

Here I used a pale green emulsion paint that I needed to use up. When thoroughly dry, and if necessary, the object can be gently sanded again and another coat of pale paint added.

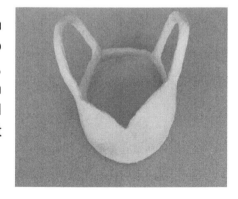

Step 12: Now paint the bra bowl in any colour and style you wish. I decided to paint this one in a "Picasso" style. I then gave it a couple of coats of varnish. Allow to dry between each coat of varnish.

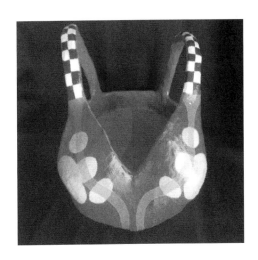

This bowl should only be used for dry items (e.g. wrapped sweets, or fruit that is not too ripe as obviously the bowl cannot be washed).

"Most people don't see the edginess in my work. They think it's all fantasy and whimsy."

Niki de St. Phalle

A busty bust, inspired by Franco-American artist Niki de St Phalle

BUSTY BUST

This bust is supposed to be for decorative purposes, but could also be used as a dress form for making your own clothes.

In addition to the basic equipment and materials you will need: a ladies' t-shirt, some medium thickness cardboard and a willing female model.

Step 1: The t-shirt should be fairly tight-fitting, high-necked and preferably cap-sleeved, however most t-shirts can be adapted. I sewed up the front v-neck of this one. T-shirts with short sleeves can be cut near the shoulder at an angle. Baggy t-shirts can be nipped in at the waist.

For this project I cut the bottom edge off the t-shirt making the total length from top to bottom approximately 19 inches (48 cms). I left half an inch (approx 1 cm) over for attaching to the cardboard later on.

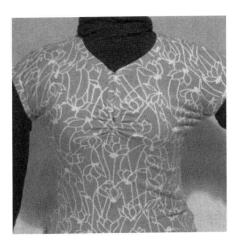

Step 2: Ask your frightened female guinea pig to model the t-shirt and make her a nice cup of tea!

Step 3: Cover the entire t-shirt with tape. Here I used parcel-packing tape, which is reasonably robust. If you use masking tape you will need more than one layer of tape as it is fairly flimsy. Duct tape is the most efficient but it is quite expensive and the idea here is to keep costs down and use whatever you have to hand.

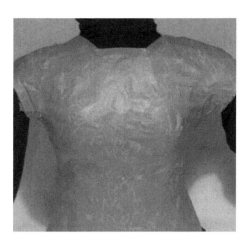

Step 4: Now, using scissors, carefully cut a slit from top to bottom (the whole way) at the back of the t-shirt.

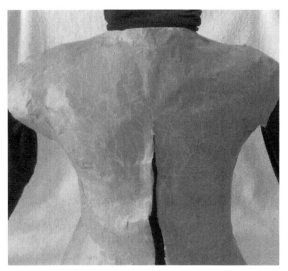

The t-shirt can now be carefully removed and the slit sealed back together with some tape.

Step 5: In the next stage you will need to insert some pieces of cardboard into the bottom (waist) edge and armholes.

Measure the width of the t-shirt at the lower edge so that you can calculate how big the piece of cardboard for the bottom needs to be.

The width on mine was 17.5 inches (44.50cms), so X 2 that will make a 35 inch (89cms) circumference (and slightly oval). Measure the width of the arm holes and, once again, multiply the measurement by 2.

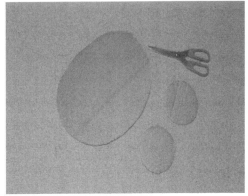

Using your measurements, draw the shapes onto some cardboard and cut them out. You will need an oval for the bottom and two smaller circles for the arm holes

Step 6: Insert and tape the large piece of cardboard into the bottom of the t-shirt. Then insert and tape the two smaller pieces of cardboard into the armholes.

Stand the t-shirt upright and stuff the inside tightly with newspaper. Alternatively you can stuff with lightweight plastic bags, paper bags, receipts, old bills, and letters, worn out socks or printed computer paper. Nothing too thick or bulky though and all must be clean and food free.

It is quite amazing how much rubbish you can get rid of in this way. Stuff to just below the neck hole. A long thin stick or knitting needle can be used to gently push the stuffing into empty remote areas. Be careful not to push too hard otherwise you risk breaking through the tape.

Step 7: Once stuffed, you will now need to close the neck hole of the t-Shirt.

Measure, draw and cut out 2 pieces of cardboard.

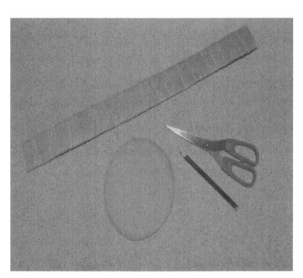

One should be a long thin piece which is the circumference of the neck opening X 2 inches (5cms) width.

The other should be a small circle (circumference of the neck) to insert into and cover the top of the neck opening.

Step 8: When the t-shirt is almost fully stuffed, attach the long piece of cardboard around the perimeter of the neck hole to form a neck. Fix securely with tape.

Continue stuffing the neck area right to the top until it is crammed full.

Step 9: When fully stuffed, tape the cardboard round lid onto the top of the neck. This is now ready for covering with strips

Step 10: Cover the entire bust with paper strips. A couple of layers should be sufficient.

When dry, lay the object down and cover the underside with paper strips too.

Step 11: Now start to cover the entire object with paper pulp. This stage is entirely optional as if you wish you can just continue with paper strips until you feel the object is solid enough (usually 8–10 layers).

Personally I like to use the pulp to smooth out any uneven areas, cover mistakes, holes, lumps and bumps.

The breast area can also be enlarged at this stage if you wish. You can truly sculpt your object with the pulp.

Step 12: Once the object is covered in pulp and has thoroughly dried, give the whole object a light sanding, and paint on a base coat in a pale colour.

Use cheap emulsion or acrylic paint. Use up old wall paint.

It is now ready for decorating.

Step 13: Now you have the pleasure of decorating your bust.

I painted one in a Niki de St Phalle style and another I "decoupaged" with some vintage magazine images.

"The purpose – where I start – is the idea of use. It is not recycling, it's reuse."

Issey Miyake

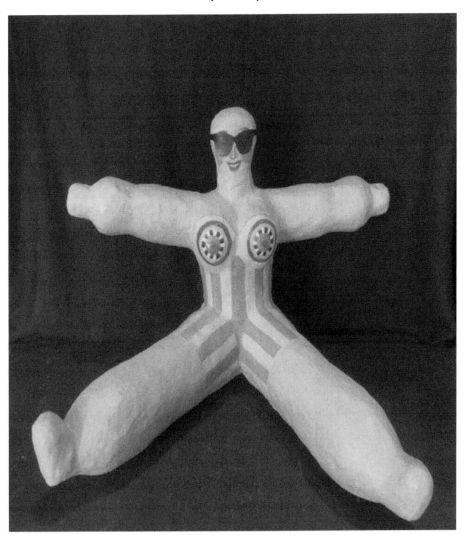

Plastic Bottle Beach Babe, inspired by artist Niki de St Phalle

PLASTIC BOTTLE BEACH BABE

This cute art doll is fairly easy to undertake and a great way of using up plastic water bottles.

In addition to the equipment mentioned in Equipment and Materials you will need: two small plastic water bottles, two larger water bottles, one medium sized plastic water or plastic milk bottle, a small rounded jar (e.g. Marmite jar or similar) and some silver foil.

Try to use rounded bottles; some are a bit too angular. Bottles with a few curves in them are ideal and it is quite fun to choose bottles and jars accordingly when you go shopping.

Step 1: I recommend first filling the bottles with small pieces of paper, card or plastic. This not only gives some weight to the doll (especially to the body and legs) to make it more robust, but it is also an excellent way to incorporate even more household waste into your project.

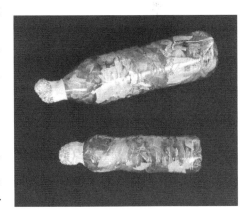

Doing this helps towards our zero waste goal.

Everything I used as stuffing was clean and then chopped up using scissors or torn by hand. A long thin object, such as a knitting needle, can be used to push the pieces down.

Step 2: Tape the two larger water bottles (the legs) to the medium milk bottle (the body).

Step 3: Tape the two smaller water bottles (the arms) to the sides of the milk bottle (the body) and the small jar to the top of the body to form the head and neck.

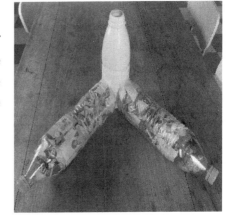

For the head I used a small upturned Marmite jar, which was perfect. Alternatively, a small round jam jar, a ball, a door knob, the head of a discarded toy or other similar object can be used.

Hands and feet can be made by scrunching some foil (or newspaper) into the shapes of little hands and feet and then taping these to the ends of the legs and the arms. I try not to use new foil. I save old clean pieces in a bag ready for use.

Step 4: As the art doll is female you will also need to give her a few curves, unless, of course, you decide to make a male bottle babe.

To construct the bust and buttocks, line a large tea strainer or other similar concave object with foil, leaving a bit extra over the edges. Next, stuff this makeshift mould with small pieces of newspaper. Once this is filled, close the top using the excess foil and use some tape to seal.

I used two different sizes of tea strainer for mine: a larger one for the buttocks and a smaller one for the breasts.

Step 5: These little half moon shapes can then be attached to the top of the milk bottle at the front to form the bust (the two smaller half moons) and at the bottom of the milk bottle at the lower back to form the buttocks (two larger half moons).

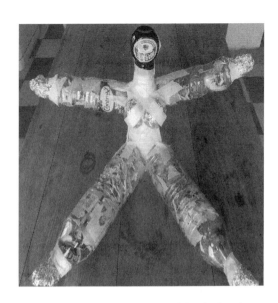

Step 6: Once you have made and added the bust and buttocks cover the entire object with 5 – 8 layers of paper strips. You will need to wait for the topside of the legs to dry before you turn her over to complete the undersides of the legs and buttocks, then dry upside down.

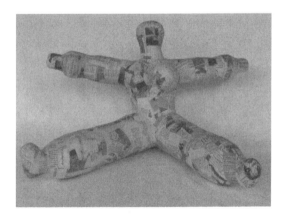

You should now have a little paper person that roughly resembles the photo (above). Now give this a light sanding with very fine sandpaper and she is ready for painting.

Step 7: Apply a coat of light coloured paint as a base coat.

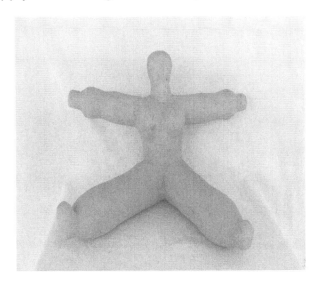

Step 8: Paint her in flashy colours. Again, I have used a Niki de St Phalle style design for her swim suit.

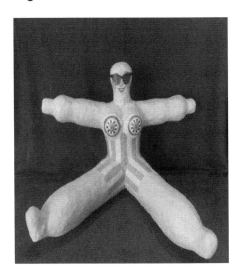

Once your design is dry, give the object a couple of coats of acrylic varnish.

"Art is not what you see, but what you make others see."

Edgar Degas.

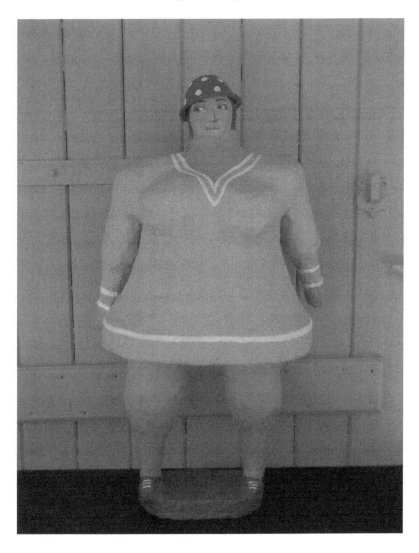

Naif Art Doll, inspired by a lampshade!

NAÏF ART DOLL

I cannot resist thinking up characters based on objects lying around the house. My garden shed is full of bits and bobs waiting to become little characters. In mixing a few objects together I came up with this little lady.

For this project, in addition to the basic equipment and materials, I used: beer bottles, an old lamp shade, plastic water bottles, a plastic detergent bottle, a plastic tub (ice cream container), a plastic yoghurt pot and some old bamboo sticks from the garden.

Step 1: Fill the ice cream tub with some Plaster of Paris and before completely dry insert two thin sticks (e.g. bamboo sticks). Push them right to the bottom of the tub and next to the outside edges (as below).

The sticks should be approximately 12 to 18 inches (30cms to 46cms) for 1.5 liter bottles.

Step 2: Add two upturned large plastic bottles and tape in place onto the sticks.

Tape the bottles together at the top where the thighs would be, so there is no gap, and also around the ankle area to attach to the sticks.

Step 3: Insert and tape an old lamp shade on to the bottles, taping the bottles to the metal structure on the inside of the lampshade.

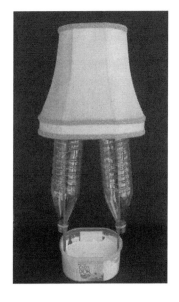

This will form the skirt part of the dress.

Step 4: Take a large plastic detergent bottle and cut it into two. Keep the bottom half for a future project, or use it as your glue container.

Step 5: Insert the top half of the detergent bottle into the lamp shade skirt to form the torso, shoulders and neck. Secure with lots of tape.

Step 6: For the arms I taped on some upside down beer bottles to either side of the detergent bottle torso.

Tape everything together securely.

Step 7: Cover the whole item (except the base) with 2 or 3 layers of paper mache strips.

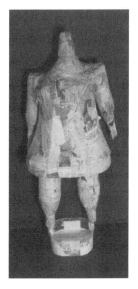

I decided I preferred the arms swinging back rather than forward, but you can do either.

Step 8: Scrunch up some newspaper into a ball and tape to the neck area to form a head.

Gently cut the plastic ice cream container away leaving the exposed Plaster of Paris stand.

Step 9: Scrunch up some more pieces of newspaper and tape to the shoulders to form them and pad them out a bit. If you wish your doll to have a bust, add some more scrunched balls of paper to the torso to form breasts (or use tea-strainer method used in Bottle Babe).

I also made some little hands and feet with some scrunched up foil, which I taped on to ends of the arms and legs, as seen above.

Step 10: Cover your new scrunched paper and foil areas with more paper strips.

Step 11: I expect you want to know what is going on under the skirt. I stuffed the interior with screwed up newspaper, covered over the whole area with tape and then applied paper strips over that.

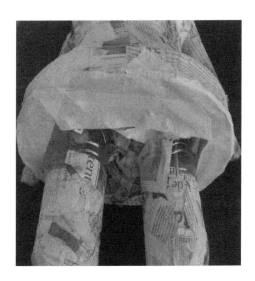

Step 12: Either continue to add several more layers of paper strips or apply a layer of paper pulp.

Step 13: Once your paper pulp or paper strips are dry, she is ready for sanding and painting. Sand lightly and give her a coat of pale paint as an undercoat.

Step 14: I made a hat by covering a plastic yoghurt pot (below) with some paper strips.

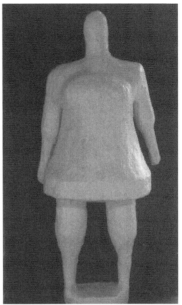

Step 16: I painted the face pale pink and then cut some hair and facial features from a magazine advert and glued them over the top of the pink paint.

Step 17: I painted the whole sculpture including the hat, and gave her a couple of coats of varnish.

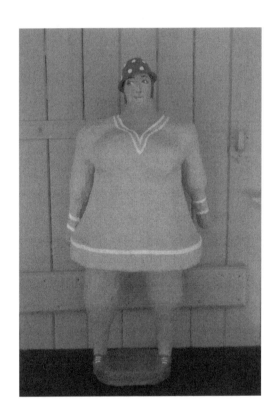

I feel like she is missing a dog and a handbag, so that will be a future project!

"Good artists copy, great artists steal."

Pablo Picasso

Bowl with Picasso style design

PICASSO BOWL

How often do you break things at home? Do not despair and do not throw them away! They can be repaired, rebuilt and reinvented.

I managed to break a brand new plastic salad bowl, but rather than throw it out I decided to repair it and transform it into a jazzy paper mâché fruit bowl.

In addition to the basic materials for this project you will need a bowl, any type, (broken, cracked or old) and some thick cardboard.

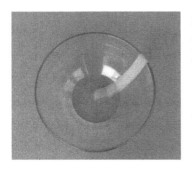

Step 1: Repair the chips or cracks in your bowl, (or plate, cup, other item) with some masking tape.

Here there was just one crack down the whole side of the bowl.

If you have an actual separate broken piece just insert and tape it back on.

This project can be used for broken ceramic/wooden objects too.

Step 2: Cover the entire object inside and out with 2–3 layers of paper strips.

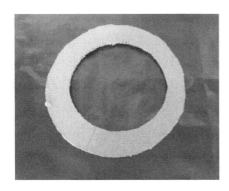

Step 3: To make it a little more interesting I added a rim by measuring the circumference at the top (of the inner rim) and then cutting out a circle of thick cardboard 2 inches (5cms) deep and taping it on to the bowl.

Cover the rim both sides with two layers of paper strips whilst at the same time overlapping the strips onto the edge of the bowl for extra security.

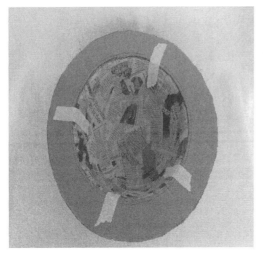

Step 4: Cover your bowl with a layer of pulp or paper strips.

For strips about 8–10 layers will be needed to make it nice and sturdy.

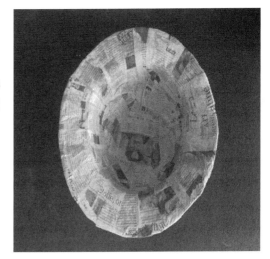

Step 5: Once dry, the bowl is ready to paint.

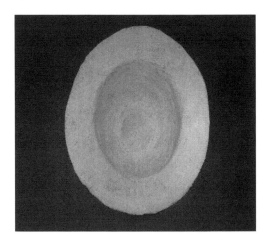

Give it a light sanding and add a base coat using pale coloured wall emulsion or acrylic paint.

Step 6: I painted my bowl with acrylic colours, using a contemporary Picasso style design.

I then finished it off with a couple of layers of varnish.

"Recycle like there's no tomorrow."
Earth Day Quote

Inspired by an Orangina bottle!

JUGGLING CLOWN

Not a toy, but a joyful object to have on display in your home. Mine always brings a smile to my face.

In addition to the basic equipment and materials for this project you will need an old empty paint tin, a jar, 4 small bottles (e.g. Perrier or Orangina), some thin card (e.g. cereal packet), some stones or sand, old golf balls (or similar).

Step 1: For the base I used a medium sized paint tin. This one is approximately 11cms across by 14cms high.

Fill the tin to the top with sand or stones or other heavy objects that you no longer need. Replace the lid and secure the top with some masking tape.

Step 2: Cover the tin with one layer of paper strips.

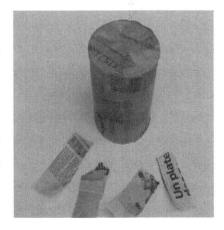

Allow the tin to dry thoroughly as you will be taping objects to the surface.

Step 3: Once dry, tape one of the bottles on to the base to make a leg. The bottle should be upside down to give the best shape. You may need some help at this stage to hold the bottle whilst you tape it on. Make sure it is nice and secure.

Here I used a small Perrier bottle as I liked the shape.

Step 4: Cover the bottle and the tin entirely with another layer of paper strips.

Allow to dry. Paper mache can take a long time to dry especially on a cold day in an unheated room. In the summer I like to dry in the sun, but away from animals and children.

Step 5: Once properly dry, added some more tape to the bottom of the leg to make sure it is fully secure. Wind some masking tape around the ankle for extra force. Using some scrunched up silver foil or newspaper, make a little foot and tape it down onto the lid in front of the leg.

58

Cover the taped area with some more paper strips, using smaller strips for the foot. Leave to dry, or use a hair dryer to speed up the process.

Step 6: Next, tape a smallish jam jar on to the top of the leg to form a body. The jar I used fitted neatly over the bottom of the bottle (it was approximately 12cm high by 6cm across). If you find it is not a snug fit, use a different jar or turn the jar up the other way.

The jar will form the hips and lower torso of the clown. Cover the jar and the bottle with another layer of paper strips and leave to dry.

Step 7: Next, using a small piece of cardboard, make the bottom of the flared trouser leg and tape it round the base of the leg above the foot.

For this I used the edge of a paper plate, but any thin cardboard will do.

Step 8: On the left side of the leg, near the foot, tape on an old golf ball, small ball or other round object.

If you do not have a ball, scrunched up foil or newspaper is fine. Cover the ball, trouser bottom and taped areas with a layer of small paper strips.

Step 9: Now add a thin layer of paper pulp to the leg and lower body. If you do not wish to use paper pulp, you can also achieve a sturdy frame just by applying lots of layers (at least 8) of paper strips.

When totally covered leave to dry in an area where there is as much circulating warm air as possible. The drying process for pulp can take many hours so ideally leave to dry at least overnight.

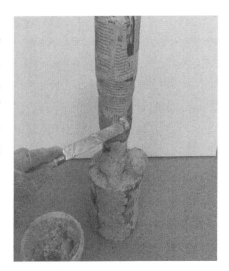

Step 10: Once the pulp is thoroughly dry, attach another bottle onto the structure at a slight angle. You may need help with this. It can be fiddly.

This second bottle will form the right leg.

Step 11: Fill the gap at the top of the right leg (the hip area) with small pieces of screwed up newspaper.

Make a little foot at the bottom of the right leg with foil or screwed up newspaper. Secure with tape. Cover the gap at the top of the leg and the foil foot with more tape, and then cover the whole right leg (including foot) and taped areas with more paper strips.

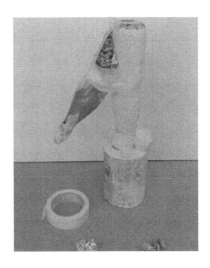

Step 12: Once covered and dry, tape two bottles together, underside to underside, and then tape them onto the lower torso to form the upper part of the body and arms.

Here I used two glass Orangina bottles.

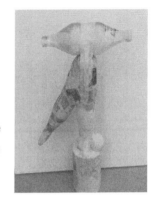

Step 13: Next form a trouser bottom for the right leg with cardboard, using the same method used earlier for the left leg.

Scrunch up some small pieces of foil or newspaper and insert into the bottle openings at the end of each arm to make some little hands.

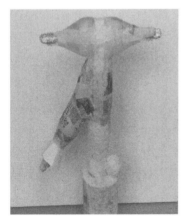

Secure everything well with masking tape and cover these areas with more paper mache strips and allow to dry.

Step 14: Tape an old golf ball onto a plastic bottle top to form a head and neck, and then tape the whole thing to the top of the body.

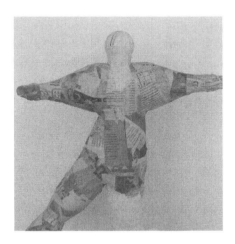

If you do not have a golf ball, ball or bottle top, use scrunched up paper or foil (for head) and thin cardboard (for neck) instead.

Alternatively an old round door knob can also be used to form the head and neck.

Step 15: Add a triangular hat to the head using some cardboard.

Here I used an individual teabag holder. If you don't have a similar teabag holder, make a hat by employing the same method as you used for making the trouser bottom earlier. Or cut 4 triangular shapes from thin cardboard (e.g. cereal packet) and tape them together to make the pointy hat.

Tape a golf ball (or similar) onto the left arm for one of the juggling balls. If desired, a further 2 balls can be added to the right arm and right ankle, or add as many balls as you wish. Cover these areas with more paper strips.

Step 16: Now add a thin layer of paper pulp to all these areas except the left leg (which has already been covered) and the tin (not necessary). (Please see instructions in Techniques chapter for paper pulp method).

Fill any holes or gaps using the mixture, and pad out areas with the pulp if you wish. Once the pulp is spread on I like to smooth the surface over with my fingers (in gloves), which cuts down on the amount of sanding I will have to do at the end.

Step 17: Once the sculpture is dry, and preferably wearing a protective face mask, sand over any lumps and bumps or creases with fine sandpaper.

Step 18: Apply a layer of undercoat using a light coloured emulsion or acrylic paint. Here I used some pale green paint left over from a bedroom project.

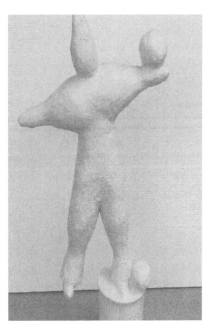

Allow to dry in between each layer of paint and sand again if necessary.

Step 19: Draw the outline of the clown costume in pencil, and then paint in your design using the colours of your choice. You may need to use two layers of paint for perfect coverage.

Clowns can be as jazzy and bright as you like.

Be adventurous!

Step 20: When your design is finished, paint on a couple of layers of varnish and allow to dry in between each layer.

For best results apply the varnish thinly and slowly to avoid drips as this can ruin the finished product.

"Every artist was first an amateur."

Ralph Waldo Emerson

ABOUT THE AUTHOR

I have been working with, and fascinated by, paper mache for many years. It is my method of relaxation and meditation and I find it enormously rewarding.

I love the spirit of "mend and make do" and tend to see art and potential in every discarded, broken or unloved object. Yes, EVERY object. From an old toothless comb to a squashed, rusty tin can, to a yellowing brazier. They are all beautiful in my eyes. What a shame to let them go to landfill sites and recycling centres when they could easily be given a new lease of life, indeed a much better life, in the form of beautiful works of art or useful objects for the home.

The possibilities are just endless....

Printed in Great Britain
by Amazon